The Butter

by Ruth Renolo
illustrated by Gina McGee

PEARSON

Scott
Foresman

Editorial Offices: Glenview, Illinois • Parsippany, New Jersey • New York, New York
Sales Offices: Needham, Massachusetts • Duluth, Georgia • Glenview, Illinois
Coppell, Texas • Ontario, California • Mesa, Arizona

Every effort has been made to secure permission and provide appropriate credit for photographic material. The publisher deeply regrets any omission and pledges to correct errors called to its attention in subsequent editions.

Unless otherwise acknowledged, all photographs are the property of Scott Foresman, a division of Pearson Education.

Photo locators denoted as follows: Top (T), Center (C), Bottom (B), Left (L), Right (R), Background (Bkgd)

Illustrations by Ginna Magee

ISBN: 0-328-13277-2

2 3 4 5 6 7 8 9 10 V0G1 14 13 12 11 10 09 08 07 06 05

It's summer. So Mama and I visit Nana.

Nana has lemonade for us. I drink my lemonade. Then I go play with things I find in two of Nana's old trunks.

I play dress-up with the old clothes in one of the trunks. Last time, I dressed up and pretended to be a queen.

The other trunk is full of quilts. They are wrapped up in blankets. I like the bright butterfly quilt the best.

Nana helps me get it unpacked. She tells the story about how it was made. She tells about the different people that the butterfly shapes represent.

"This quilt was made by your great-great-grandmother Nell," Nana says.

"First, Nell saved pieces from old clothes. Next, she cut the pieces into the shapes of butterfly wings.

"Then, she sewed two pairs of wings on a square of cloth. Last, she stitched on black antennae and a long body.

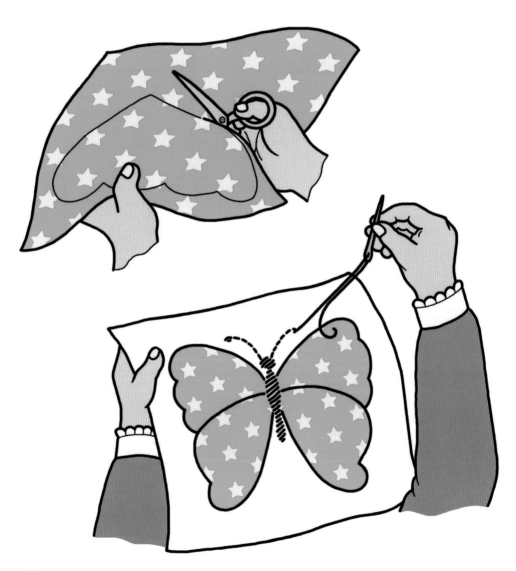

"When Nell had lots of butterfly squares, she stitched them all together into one big piece. After that, she stitched the butterfly piece to a plain sheet. She put soft stuffing inside. It took her a long time to finish the quilt."

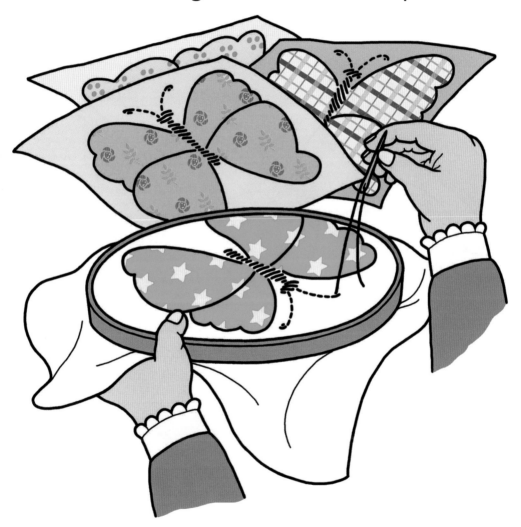

Nana points to the quilt. She says, "This butterfly was made from an old plaid shirt that Nell's father wore in the store. This other butterfly came from a bandana your great-great-grandfather wore on his farm.

"This one came from a dress my mother wore," Nana said. "This flower print came from Great-aunt Bella's curtains. This blue stripe came from Great-uncle Bob's baseball uniform."

I help Nana pack the quilt away after she tells us the butterfly quilt story. Then it's time for Mama and me to go home.

On our way home, I tell Mama, "I think we should make a quilt for our part of the family. Then, someday you can tell a quilt story to your grandchildren."

Native American Quilts

Many Native American families make special quilts. Some quilts are handed down in families to help tell family stories. They are offered as gifts at weddings, births, funerals, and tribal meetings.

Star shapes have special meaning for many Native Americans. The patterns are made from small diamond shapes. They are cut from plain, brightly colored material. The shapes are pieced together into a star shape, sometimes called the morning star pattern.